THE UNIVERSE

Venus

Revised and Updated

Tim Goss

Heinemann Library
Chicago, Illinois

Customer Service 888-454-2279

Visit our website at www.heinemannraintree.com

Photo research by Mica Brancic
Designed by Richard Parker and Tinstar Design www.tinstar.co.uk
Illustrations by Calvin J. Hamilton
Printed in China by Leo Paper Group

12 11 10 09 08
10 9 8 7 6 5 4 3 2 1

New edition ISBNs: 9781432901721 (hardback)

9781432901844 (paperback)

The Library of Congress has cataloged the first edition as follows:

Goss, Tim, 1958-

Venus / by Tim Goss.

v. cm. -- (The universe)

Includes bibliographical references and index.

ISBN 1-58810-919-4 (HC), 1-4034-0620-0 (Pbk)

1. Venus (Planet)--Juvenile literature. [1. Venus (Planet)] I.Title. II. Series.

QB621 .G67 2002

523.42--dc21

2002000812

Acknowledgments

The author and publisher are grateful to the following for permission to reproduce copyright material: p. 4 John Foster/Photo Researchers, Inc.; p. 5 NASA/Ames Research Center/Rick Guidice; p. 6. D. Van Ravenswaay/Photo Researchers, Inc.; p. 7 L. Esposito/University of Colorado, Boulder, and NASA; pp. 8, 10 Bettman/Corbis; p. 9 Science Photo Library/Dan Schechter; pp. 11, 16, 17, 18 19, 28, 29 NASA/JPL/Caltech; p. 12 Ecoscene/Corbis; p. 13 NASA/JPL; p. 14 NASA/U.S. Geological Survey; pp. 15, 20 Courtesy of Calvin J. Hamilton/ www.solarviews.com; pp. 21, 23, 24, 25 NASA/National Space Science Data Center; pp. 22, 26 NASA/Kennedy Space Center; p. 27 European Space Agency/D. Ducros

Cover photograph by Getty Images/PhotoDisc

The publishers would like to thank Geza Gyuk of the Adler Planetarium, Chicago, for his assistance in the preparation of this book.

Contents

Any words appearing in the text in bold, **like this**,
are explained in the Glossary.

Where in the Sky Is Venus?

Venus is always near the Sun, and it rises and sets with the Sun. Depending on where it is in its **orbit** around the Sun, Venus can be the first object you see in the sky when the Sun sets. Other times it can be seen just before sunrise. Some ancient **astronomers** thought they were seeing two different **stars.** They called them the Evening Star and the Morning Star. Today we know that Venus is one **planet**, not two stars.

Venus is the brightest planet in the night sky. From Earth, the only thing brighter is the Moon. Sometimes it is even bright enough to cast shadows on the ground. Venus usually can be seen without a **telescope.** If you use a telescope on a night when Venus can be seen in the dark sky, Venus appears as a yellow-white ball. You can occasionally see Venus during the day if you know where to look.

In this photo, the planets Venus, Mars, and Jupiter appear at sunset in the sky over Utah.

Venus is the second closest planet to the Sun and is Earth's closest neighbor.

The solar system

The **solar system** is made of everything that circles the Sun: planets, **comets**, **asteroids**, and other objects. The Sun's **gravity** pulls on all of the objects in our solar system. If it were not for the pull of the Sun, the planets would travel in straight lines. This would send them out into deep space! The force of gravity keeps the planets in regular paths around the Sun called orbits.

Mercury is the only planet that is closer to the Sun than Venus. At times, Venus is only 26 million miles (42 million kilometers) from Earth. This may seem like a large distance. But think about the planet Neptune—it is more than 100 times further from Earth than Venus is.

How did Venus get its name?

Venus is the only planet in our solar system that is named after a female. The ancient Greeks and the Romans named the planet after the goddess of beauty and love. The Greeks called her Aphrodite and the Romans called her Venus.

How does Venus move through the sky?

A **year** on a **planet** is the time it takes for the planet to make one **orbit** around the Sun. A Venus year lasts about 225 Earth **days.** The orbit of Venus around the Sun is the second shortest orbit of any planet in the **solar system.** Only Mercury has a shorter orbit than Venus.

Venus moves around the Sun at a distance of about 67 million miles (108 million kilometers). Earth travels around the Sun at a distance of about 93 million miles (150 million kilometers).

A Venus day

A day on a planet is the amount of time it takes to spin around on its **axis**, the imaginary line through the center of a planet from its north pole to its south pole. It takes Venus 243 Earth days to do this. Earth takes about 24 hours, or one Earth day, to spin around on its axis.

Venus spins much more slowly on its axis than Earth. Because Venus spins so slowly on its axis and has a short orbit around the Sun, a Venus day is longer than a Venus year!

Early studies of Venus

Ancient Greek **astronomers** first thought that Venus was two different objects. One object seemed to appear at sunset, and the other seemed to appear at sunrise. Through the 1500s, people did not know much about Venus. Sometimes the bright planet scared sailors as they sailed at sunset. From far away on the **horizon,** Venus looked like a bright enemy ship on the water!

The famous astronomer Galileo Galilei discovered that Venus had **phases** like our Moon. He also discovered that Venus travels in an orbit around the Sun. This was big news! Most people at the time thought everything in space moved around Earth. Galileo said that Venus was closer to the Sun than Earth. This made people think that maybe the Sun was the center of the system of planets and **stars**.

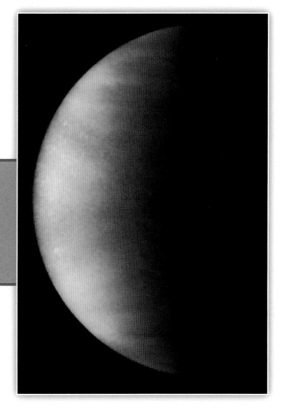

False color was added to this image to show Venus's cloud features more clearly.

For many years, astronomers thought Venus might be just like Earth. They had learned that it was about the same size as Earth, and it was our closest neighbor planet. This made scientists think Venus might be made of the same material as Earth. Maybe it was even "born" at about the same time as our planet.

Why Does Venus Look Yellow?

Venus is completely covered by a thick layer of pale, yellowish white clouds. We cannot see the surface of Venus through a **telescope** because of all the clouds.

What are Venus's clouds made of?

The clouds of Venus are made of small drops of a poisonous liquid called **sulfuric acid.** This acid is the liquid used in car batteries. The cloud layer on Venus is 12.5 miles (20 kilometers) thick.

The atmosphere of Venus

Venus has a very thick **atmosphere,** but you would not be able to breathe there. The atmosphere is made of **carbon dioxide.** That is the gas we breathe out, not in. There is a small amount of **nitrogen** in Venus's atmosphere, but we cannot breathe that, either. We need oxygen to breathe. There is no oxygen at all on Venus.

The atmosphere has different layers in it. The layer closest to the surface of Venus is 10 miles (16 kilometers) thick. It is made mostly of carbon dioxide gas and small amounts of nitrogen gas. This inner layer of the atmosphere looks mostly clear, but it traps heat from the Sun. This causes extremely high temperatures on the surface of Venus. If you tried to build a home on Venus, the home would burn up very quickly!

Thick clouds move quickly across the surface of Venus.

What Is Special About Venus?

Venus spins backward! Venus and all the other **planets** and **moons** in our **solar system** spin as they move through space. Imagine an invisible line running through the middle of a planet or moon from top to bottom. This line is called an **axis.** Earth's axis runs from the North Pole to the South Pole. Our planet spins around its axis in a west to east direction, left to right. That is why the Sun first appears in the east every morning. At night, it sets and disappears in the west.

Venus spins in the opposite direction. It rotates from east to west, right to left. We call this **retrograde rotation.** Venus is the only planet that does this. If you were flying above the clouds on Venus, you would see that the Sun rises each **day** in the west and sets in the east. That's the opposite of how the Sun rises and sets when viewed from Earth. This difference is because of Venus's retrograde rotation.

After the Moon, Venus is the brightest object in the night skies. It is so bright that it can cast shadows. Venus is never more than about 45 degrees from the Sun so it can only be seen at dawn or dusk.

Venus is the brightest planet

When **astronomers** look at Venus, it is always very bright. All **planets** and **moons** can be seen because they reflect the Sun's light. Venus shines more brightly than all the other planets because of its thick clouds. Many of the Sun's light rays bounce off the clouds instead of going through them. This makes Venus look very bright.

Venus is also bright because of its place in the **solar system.** Venus is much closer to the Sun than Earth. More light from the Sun reaches Venus than Earth. If you were standing on Venus, the Sun would shine almost twice as brightly as it does on Earth.

The color filters used for this image of Venus show the cloud features of the upper **atmosphere**.

What's the Weather Like on Venus?

The weather on Venus is about the same almost every **day.** Gentle breezes blow at about 2 to 4 miles (3.2 to 6.4 kilometers) per hour near the surface. It is always hot and dry. The surface has a temperature of 870°F (465°C). That is hotter than the highest temperature setting for your oven at home. Nothing can live on a planet with such high temperatures. No **space probe** on Venus has ever lasted more than a couple of hours before melting and falling apart.

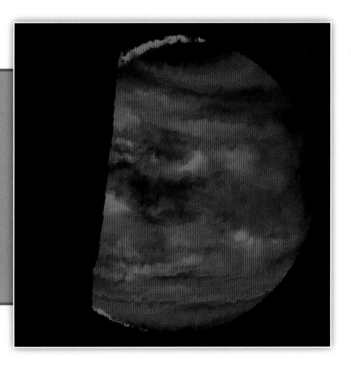

The red color in this image represents the heat levels coming from the lower atmosphere of Venus. The bright slivers are high clouds reflecting sunlight.

Venus is the hottest planet in our **solar system**. It is even hotter than Mercury, which is closer to the Sun. That is because the thick, dense **atmosphere** of Venus acts like a huge blanket. Only a small amount of the Sun's energy can get through the clouds, but then it cannot get back out. This is like what happens in a greenhouse on Earth, only much stronger. We call this the **greenhouse effect.**

How does the greenhouse effect work?

Have you ever stepped into a car that had its windows and doors shut and had been sitting in the hot sunlight for many hours? It feels like you are stepping into a giant oven. The heat that you feel inside of the car comes from the sunlight. The Sun's rays carry light and heat energy. They pass easily through the car windows. The windows act like a one-way door for the heat. It is easy to enter but very hard to leave!

Scientists call this the **greenhouse effect.** In a greenhouse, sunlight passes through the glass windows and helps plants to grow. The heat from the Sun's rays cannot escape, so the temperature inside slowly rises. The **atmosphere** of Venus has a thick layer of clouds and a thick layer of **carbon dioxide** gas. These layers act just like the windows on a car or greenhouse. They let the Sun's rays pass into the atmosphere, but they do not let the heat escape easily from the atmosphere. Venus has a lot more carbon dioxide in its atmosphere than Earth has, so a lot more heat gets trapped on Venus. Because of the clouds and carbon dioxide gas, temperatures on Venus are very hot during both the day and the night.

Plants inside a greenhouse have a controlled environment and are more likely to grow well. The glass walls trap in heat.

Thick clouds

Due to Venus's cloud layer, we cannot use ordinary **telescopes** to study the surface of Venus from outside its atmosphere. Scientists first used **radar** to learn about the surface of Venus. Special radio telescopes send radar signals to Venus. The way these signals bounce back to Earth gives scientists information about the surface, **atmospheric pressure,** and other things about the **planet.** Radio signals can also be sent from antennas on Earth or from satellites that **orbit** Earth. After scientists first studied Venus with radar, **space probes** from the United States and Russia took a closer look at the planet on **flyby** missions.

This image of Venus, seen from the *Magellan* space probe, shows the surface of the planet, which is usually hidden by clouds.

Crushing pressure

The atmospheric pressure on Venus is 90 times greater than it is on Earth. That is the same amount of pressure that you would find about a half mile (0.9 kilometers) underwater in the ocean. Imagine how heavy all that water above and around you would feel. The atmosphere on Venus would make you feel the same way.

What Would I See if I Went to Venus?

If you ever went to Venus, you would see that its surface changes from one area to the next. There is no dirt or soil as we know it on Earth. The surface is mostly cracks and **lava plains.** There is also dust that is blown around by the wind. There may be sand dunes. In some areas, there are lots of small volcanoes gathered together like flowers in a field.

For hundreds of years, we did not know as much about Venus. The invention of the **telescope** helped **astronomers** to see objects in outer space much better. Seeing the surface of Venus has always been very hard because of the **planet's** thick clouds. In the 1950s, scientists began to use **radar** to study the planets. Starting in the 1960s, Russia and the United States sent **space probes** that used radar to study Venus.

In 1980, NASA sent a space probe from the *Pioneer* spaceship to look closer at Venus. It circled Venus many times. Its radar machine bounced signals off of the planet's surface.

This image is color-coded to show the high and low points on Venus's surface.

Venus has about 850 **craters** and giant canyons called **chasma.**
There are no small craters on Venus. Scientists think this is because
small **meteors** cannot reach the surface of Venus. They burn up in
the **atmosphere** before they hit the ground. The areas around the
craters are covered with lots of broken pieces of rocks. If you took
a walk in any of these areas, you would be walking on hardened
lava, without much dirt or soil to cover up the rocks. The lava comes
from the many volcanoes on Venus. The planet has about 430 large
volcanoes and tens of thousands of smaller ones.

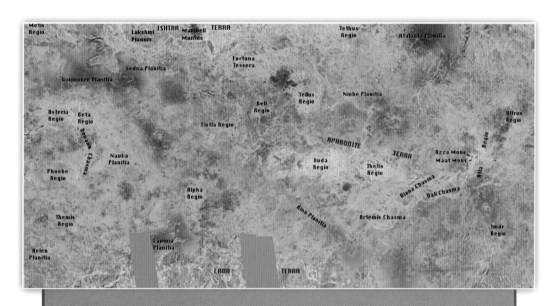

Different regions on the surface of Venus are labeled on this map.
The two gray stripes are areas that have not yet been mapped.

About 70 percent of the surface of Venus is made of rolling, desert
ground called plains. The plains have flat areas, small hills, and
valleys. Another 20 percent is flat land at a lower level than the
plains. This area is called the **lowlands.** The last 10 percent of Venus
is called the **highlands.** The highlands are regions of mountains and
flat land called **plateaus** that rise high above the plains.

Get ready to climb

Venus has three **highland** areas as big as some of Earth's **continents.** One is called Aphrodite Terra and is located near Venus's **equator.** It is about the size of the continent of South America. Another, called the Ishtar Terra region, is in the northern part of the **planet** and is about the size of Australia. The third highland area is called Lada Terra.

One of the tallest mountain ranges in our **solar system** is in the Ishtar Terra region. Some of the mountains found there—in the Maxwell Montes range—are taller than the tallest mountains on Earth. One of them, a volcano named Maat Mons, is about 7 miles (11 kilometers) high.

This is a **radar** image of Maat Mons. It is the tallest volcano in the Maxwell Montes range.

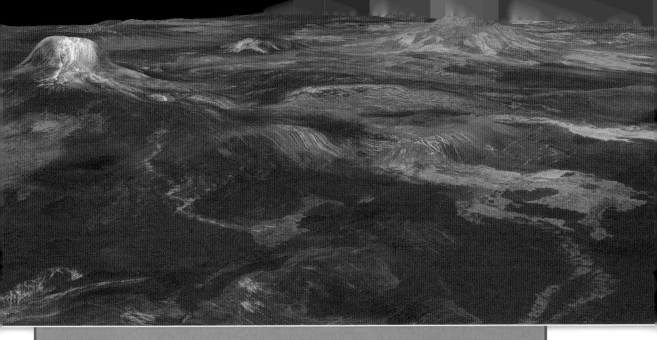

Gula Mons is the volcano to the left in this image. Sif Mons is to the right.

The **crater** at the top of the range is more than 50 miles (80 kilometers) wide. This is almost the same distance you would travel driving on a straight highway for about an hour.

Volcanoes and channels

Venus has hundreds of large volcanoes and thousands of smaller ones. **Lava** fields cover much of the **plains** and **lowlands. Channels** on Venus also tell us about the planet's volcanoes. Some channels are thousands of kilometers long. Most are about 0.6 miles (1 kilometer) wide and were probably hollowed out by flowing lava. Scientists are studying these channels to find out more about them.

Sif Mons is a mountain 1.2 miles (2 kilometers) high that was built by many separate lava flows piling up on top of each other. It is called a shield volcano. On top of Sif Mons is a **caldera** 25 to 31 miles (40 to 50 kilometers) wide. A caldera is a place where the mountaintop has sunken in after it stopped shooting out lava.

Visit a volcano

Most of the volcanic activity on Venus seems to have happened about 500 million years ago. Data from the **space probe** *Magellan* indicates that two volcanoes, Rhea Mons and Theia Mons, might still be active. There is still no direct evidence, however, to prove that the volcanoes are active.

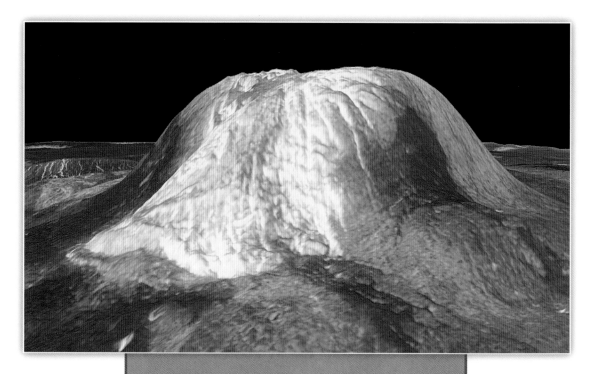

This is a closer view of Gula Mons. The volcano is 1.9 miles (3 kilometers) tall.

There are some rounded volcanoes on Venus with flat tops and steep sides. They are called pancake domes. Most pancake domes are about 0.6 miles (1 kilometer) high. They usually stretch out in a circle about 19 miles (30 kilometers) across. They get their shape when the **lava** spreads out in a circle for a short distance, then cools.

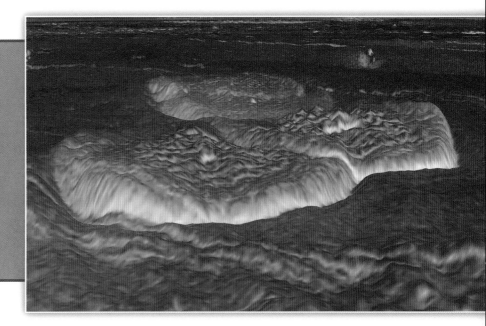

These are called pancake domes because they look like pancakes on a griddle in the **radar** photos taken from space probes.

The lava from other volcanoes on Venus spreads out over a much larger distance, so it does not create this pancake shape. Scientists do not yet know why some volcanoes form pancake domes and others do not.

How did they get their names?

Since Venus is named after a female from Roman mythology, many features on the **planet** also have female names. The tallest mountain on Venus, Maat Mons, was named for the Egyptian goddess of truth. Rhea Mons, another tall mountain on Venus, is named after a goddess of fruitfulness. Some **craters** are named after females too, including Eve, Cleopatra, and Isabella (shown here).

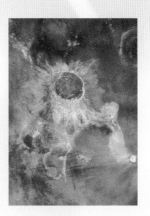

What Is Inside Venus?

Scientists cannot actually see the **core** of Venus. But from using many different types of clues, scientists think that Venus has a big core made of two types of metal—iron and nickel. Earth has the same kind of core. When a **planet** forms, the heavy and light parts melt and separate from each other. The heavy materials, like iron and other metals, sink deep into the core. The lighter materials float to the surface.

Scientists think that the core of Venus is very large, maybe even a little bigger than Earth's core. It probably stretches about 2,000 miles (3,340 kilometers) from the center of the planet.

Scientists do not know for sure, but if Venus's core is like Earth's, then the very center is solid, even though it is extremely hot. This is because of the very strong pressure. The outer core, where the pressure is lower, is probably **molten** metal.

This is an illustration of where the layers within Venus might begin and end.

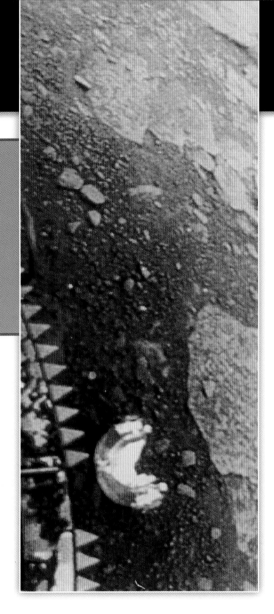

The mantle of Venus

A thick layer of rock called the **mantle** wraps around the core of Venus. It is about 1,900 miles (3,000 kilometers) thick. It starts at the edge of the core and extends to the planet's **crust**. Venus's mantle makes up most of the planet. The rocks in the mantle are partly melted, which makes it like a thick, gooey paste. The temperatures in the mantle are hot enough to soften the rocks and allow them to move slowly. The mantle gets its heat from the core and transfers it to the surface.

The crust of Venus

The crust is the outer layer of Venus. It is about 25 miles (40 kilometers) thick. It covers the entire planet and lies just above the mantle. It is very hard and much thinner than the core and the mantle. The crust is mostly made of smooth, solid **lava** rock. Venus's crust is twice as thick as Earth's crust.

Could I Ever Go to Venus?

It would be a tough trip! The thick cloud layer of Venus is made of poisonous **sulfuric acid.** This acid is very strong and it can destroy many materials. Under the clouds is a 30-mile (48-kilometer) thick **atmosphere** of **carbon dioxide** gas. You cannot breathe carbon dioxide. Temperatures here reach as high as 800°F (427°C).

Studying Venus

Since it would be so difficult for us to go to Venus, we can only look at images of the **planet**. In the 1950s, scientists began to use **radar** to learn about the surface of Venus. In the 1960s and 1970s, NASA sent *Mariner* **space probes** to study Venus. *Mariner 10* took more than 4,000 pictures of the clouds of Venus. The 1979 NASA *Pioneer-Venus* space probe used a radar machine to make a map of the surface of Venus.

Mariner 1 was launched in 1962 on a mission to **orbit** Venus.

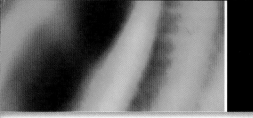

This is an artist's idea of what the *Pioneer-Venus* probe must have looked like while orbiting Venus.

Radio **telescopes** on Earth have helped map the surface of Venus. These telescopes are located in Massachusetts and California in the United States, Canberra in Australia, Arecibo in Puerto Rico, and near Madrid in Spain. Space probes provide even more details of Venus's surface than scientists were able to map using telescopes on Earth.

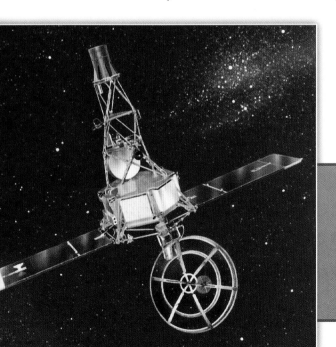

Mariner 2 went on a **flyby** mission to Venus. It was launched shortly after *Mariner 1*, which had failed shortly after its launch.

The Venera missions to Venus

Between 1961 and 1983, Russia sent many **space probes** to Venus. These trips were known as the *Venera* missions. In 1969, Russia sent *Venera 5* and *Venera 6*. Each of these space probes went through the **atmosphere** of Venus for about 52 minutes. They tested the atmosphere and sent back information as they fell toward the surface.

Venera 7 was the first space probe to reach the surface of Venus. On December 15, 1970, its tiny **lander** ship fell through the poisonous clouds of Venus. Winds of almost 250 miles (402 kilometers) per hour shook the lander as it fell toward the surface through the clouds. That wind speed is faster than the wind speed of any hurricane recorded on Earth. Winds at the base of Venus's cloud layer blow at about 90 miles (150 kilometers) per hour.

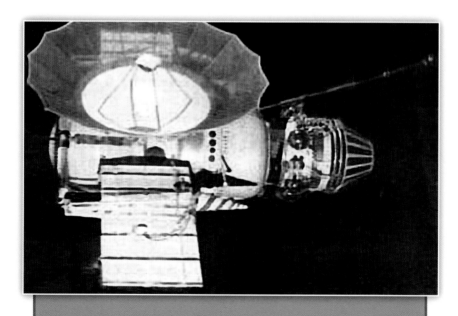

Venera 4 entered the atmosphere of Venus in 1967.

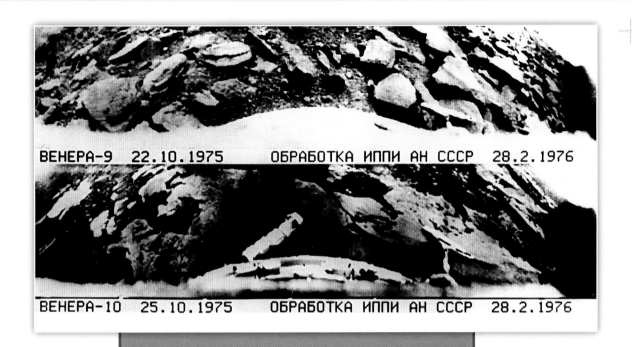

ВЕНЕРА-9   22.10.1975   ОБРАБОТКА ИППИ АН СССР   28.2.1976

ВЕНЕРА-10   25.10.1975   ОБРАБОТКА ИППИ АН СССР   28.2.1976

These were the first photos taken of Venus's surface by *Venera 9* (top) and *10* (bottom).

After passing through the clouds, the *Venera 7* lander went through a dark orange layer of gas and lightning. Then the lander crashed into the surface. During the next 23 minutes, it sent information back to Earth. Then the heat and **atmospheric pressure** on Venus destroyed the lander.

Venera 8 was designed to probe the atmosphere of Venus. It was launched in July 1972, and lasted about 50 minutes in Venus's atmosphere. The next two probes, *Venera 9* and *10,* were launched in June 1975. *Venera 9* lasted 53 minutes on Venus and sent back the first pictures of the surface. *Venera 10* lasted even longer—one hour and five minutes. Scientists learned more about the **planet** with each probe. It is now clear that humans cannot be sent to Venus because of the high temperatures and pressure.

The Magellan mission

On May 4, 1989, NASA sent the *Magellan* **space probe** toward Venus. *Magellan* took about 13 months to reach Venus. On August 10, 1989, it began to fly in an **orbit** around the bright **planet.** Every three hours and nine minutes, it made one complete trip around Venus. During each orbit, it took a **radar** photo of a different strip of ground. Each strip was about 12 miles (20 kilometers) wide and about 10,566 miles (17,000 kilometers) long. Every day *Magellan* circled Venus about eight times. By the time it finished its mission, *Magellan* had mapped almost all of the planet.

The radar images *Magellan* took of Venus were not easy to get. The radar machine sent signals through the clouds to hit the surface. When a signal bounced back, it was recorded and sent back to Earth. On Earth, scientists used powerful computers to figure out how rough and far away the surface of Venus was from the spacecraft. They used the information to make the pictures of Venus you see in this book.

The *Venus Express* probe arrived in orbit around Venus in April 2006. Scientists are using the probe to study Venus.

On October 11, 1994, the *Magellan* was sent on a crash course with Venus. Scientists did this in order to gather more information about the planet and about the spacecraft. The *Magellan* collected useful information about Venus's **atmosphere** as it traveled toward the surface. The experiment also allowed scientists to monitor how well the spacecraft handled the harsh atmospheric conditions.

Space probes have taught us a lot about Venus. But scientists hope to learn much more about Earth's closest neighbor.

Other missions to Venus

The European Space Agency (ESA) built a space probe called *Venus Express*. *Venus Express* was launched by the Russian Federal Space Agency in 2005 and reached Venus in early 2006. It is still orbiting Venus, learning about its atmosphere and clouds. The *Messenger* and *BepiColombo* space probes will also fly by Venus on their way to Mercury.

Fact File

	VENUS	EARTH
Average distance from the Sun	67 million miles (108 million kilometers)	93 million miles (150 million kilometers)
Revolution around the Sun	225 Earth days	1 Earth year (365 days)
Average speed of orbit	21.7 miles/second (35 kilometers/second)	18.6 miles/second (30 kilometers/second)
Diameter at equator	7,502 miles (12,100 kilometers)	7,909 miles (12,756 kilometers)
Time for one rotation	243 Earth days	24 hours
Atmosphere	carbon dioxide	nitrogen, oxygen
Temperature range	–49°F (–45°C) to 867°F (464°C)	–92°F (–69°C) to 136°F (58°C)

VENUS
12,100 KM
(7,502 MI)

EARTH
12,756 KM
(7,909 MI)

Venus and Earth are close in size. Earth is only slightly larger.

A trip to Venus from Earth

- When Venus and Earth come closest to each other in their **orbits,** they are 26 million miles (42 million kilometers) apart.

- Traveling by car at 70 miles (113 kilometers) per hour, the trip would take at least 42 years.

- Traveling by rocket at 7 miles (11 kilometers) per second, the trip would take at least 43 days.

More interesting facts

- Venus does not have any **moons.**

- Venus has two landforms found nowhere else in the **solar system.** Both are types of failed volcanoes. Huge bubbles of **molten** rock almost made it to the surface, but then cooled and sank again. These two landforms are called coronas, which look like crowns, and arachnids, which look like spiders.

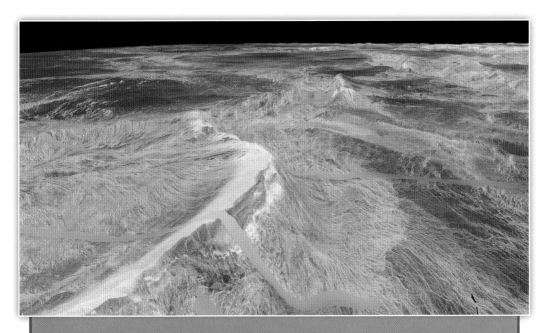

The eastern half of the Latona Corona is toward the left in this image. The rim of the corona shows up as a brighter yellow.

Glossary

asteroid large piece of floating rock that formed at the same time as the planets and orbits the Sun

astronomer person who studies objects in outer space

atmosphere all of the gases that surround an object in outer space

atmospheric pressure weight of an atmosphere

axis imaginary line through the middle of an object in space, around which it spins as it rotates

caldera place where a mountaintop has sunken in after it stopped shooting out lava

carbon dioxide heavy, colorless gas. On Earth, it is the gas we breathe out.

channel long, deep hole like a dry riverbed in the surface of a Rocky Planet

chasma very large, deep canyons in the surface of a planet

comet ball of ice and rock that orbits around the Sun

continent one of the seven large pieces of land on Earth

core center of a planet or moon

crater bowl-shaped hole in the ground that is made by a meteorite or by a burst of lava

crust top, solid layer of an object in outer space. The outer part of the crust is called the surface.

day time it takes for a planet to spin around its axis one time

equator imaginary line around the middle of a planet

flyby mission in which the spacecraft comes near to a planet but does not land

gravity force that pulls objects toward the center of an object in outer space

greenhouse effect atmosphere process in which heat from the Sun is trapped in an atmosphere by gases or clouds

highland part of the surface of a Rocky Planet that lies higher than other parts of the planet surface

horizon part of Earth where the sky and Earth seem to meet

lander small ship that leaves a space probe and flies to the surface of an object in outer space

lava melted rock from inside a planet that pours out onto the surface

lowland part of the surface of a Rocky Planet that lies deeper in the ground than other parts of the planet surface

mantle middle layer of a planet or moon. It lies between the core and the crust.

meteor piece of rock or dust that travels in outer space

molten melted into liquid form by high temperatures

moon object that floats in an orbit around a planet

nitrogen gas found in the atmosphere of Earth and some of the other planets in our solar system

orbit curved path of one object in space moving around another object

phase changing appearance of a moon or planet as it rotates. The phase is shaped by the amount of the sunlit side of the planet or moon that can be seen by the viewer.

plain large, flat surface on a Rocky Planet

planet large object in space that orbits a central star, has an atmosphere, and does not produce its own light

plateau large, flat area at a higher altitude than surface level

radar method of studying objects in which sound waves are bounced off an object to a machine that collects information about the object

retrograde rotation opposite spin of a planet or moon around its axis (it is "opposite" when compared to the direction of Earth's spin around its axis)

solar system group of objects in outer space that all float in orbits around a central star

space probe ship that carries computers and other instruments to study objects in outer space

star burning ball of gases in outer space that produces light and energy through a process of chemical change

sulfuric acid poisonous material in sulfur dioxide

telescope instrument used by astronomers to study objects in outer space

year time it takes for a planet to orbit the Sun one time; another word for *revolution*

More Books to Read

Feinstein, Stephen. *Venus.* New Jersey: Enslow, 2005.

Reinfield, R.K. *Venus.* New York: Rosen, 2004.

Simon, Charnan. *Venus.* Mankato: Child's World, 2003.

Index